S0-DQY-790

THIS IS
WHO I AM

A UNIQUE QUESTION&ANSWER
JOURNAL
FOR DISCOVERY, GROWTH,
AND SHARING WITH FRIENDS

TERRY BROWN
AND SHANNON HILL

BARBOUR
PUBLISHING

THIS IS
WHO I AM

© 2004 by Barbour Publishing, Inc.

ISBN 1-59310-186-4

All rights reserved. No part of this publication may be reproduced or transmitted in any form or by any means without written permission of the publisher.

Scripture quotations marked NIV are taken from the HOLY BIBLE, NEW INTERNATIONAL VERSION®. NIV®. Copyright © 1973, 1978, 1984 by International Bible Society. Used by permission of Zondervan Publishing House. All rights reserved.

Scripture quotations marked KJV are taken from the King James Version of the Bible.

Scripture quotations marked THE MESSAGE are from *THE MESSAGE*. Copyright © by Eugene H. Peterson 1993, 1994, 1995. Used by permission of NavPress Publishing Group.

Scripture quotations marked NKJV are taken from the New King James Version. Copyright © 1979, 1980, 1982 by Thomas Nelson, Inc. Used by permission. All rights reserved.

Scripture quotations marked NASB are taken from the New American Standard Bible, © 1960, 1962, 1963, 1968, 1971, 1972, 1973, 1975, 1977, 1995 by The Lockman Foundation. Used by permission.

Scripture quotations marked NLT are taken from the *Holy Bible*, New Living Translation, copyright © 1996. Used by permission of Tyndale House Publishers, Inc. Wheaton, Illinois 60189, U.S.A. All rights reserved.

Scripture quotations marked HCSB have been taken from the Holman Christian Standard Bible © copyright 2000 by Holman Bible Publishers. Used by permission.

All selections from *Communicate* and *I Believe* by Terry Brown and Michael Ross, © 2002 and 2003, published by Barbour Publishing, Inc., are used by permission of the authors.

Cover image © Comstock

Published by Barbour Publishing, Inc., P.O. Box 719, Uhrichsville, Ohio 44683
www.barbourbooks.com

Our mission is to publish and distribute inspirational products offering exceptional value and biblical encouragement to the masses.

Member of the
Evangelical Christian
Publishers Association

Printed in the United States of America.
5 4 3 2 1

contents

Introduction: The Why and How of Using This Book 9

Chapter 1: This Is Who I Am. 11

Chapter 2: This Is Who They Are: Family and Friends 39

Chapter 3: This Is What I Think about Love, Dating,

    and the Opposite Sex 65

Chapter 4: This Is What Fills My World 91

Chapter 5: This Is What I Believe. 115

Chapter 6: This Is Who I Want to Be. 141

My Personal Journaling. 165

My Goal List 179

My Prayer List. 180

My Contacts. 185

Sources 189

I heard an angel speak last night,
And he said, "Write!"

Elizabeth Barrett Browning

"Father, I want those you have given
me to be with me where I am,
and to see my glory,
the glory you have given me
because you loved me
before the creation of the world."

John 17:24 niv

dedication

For my mom, brothers, and sisters
tb

For Janelle
sh

the why and how of using this book

Of all the things to share with other people—gifts, money, doing good works, your time—communicating who you *really* are is probably the hardest thing to do. Why? Because it's easier for us to share with others *what we want them to think about us*, protecting our inmost thoughts, opinions, and feelings from judgment. We're afraid to let people see what's real about us, because we think that they might not like what they see inside. But our God knows every detail of our lives, and He continues to desire an intimate relationship with us.

We can't hide behind masks. Isn't it awesome that He still loves us no matter how we feel or what we do? And His love gives us the strength to share our hearts with others.

Communicate: This Is Who I Am is an interactive journal that allows you to reveal your deepest thoughts—some of which you are ready to expose to your closest friends. It's an open door to get real, get it down on paper, and let people in on your opinions, your likes and dislikes, and your true feelings. The journal encourages you to write your replies to the challenging—yet entertaining—prompts and then asks a good friend to do the same in the "My friend says" sections of the book. You'll also find relevant Scriptures, quotes, and selections from the *Communicate: I Believe* book and other awesome resources to give your mind important information and key tips to digest.

What better way to talk about the important stuff of life (and some not-so-important stuff, too), build deeper friendships, and communicate who you really are?

Discover what you didn't know about yourself, your beliefs, and your relationships with those you love.

Your feelings are valuable, and even if you are just writing for the sake of putting pen on paper, you'll be amazed at how you feel after journaling your incredible journey.

this is who I am

chapter one

My Vitals

I will praise thee; for I am fearfully
and wonderfully made:
marvellous are thy works; and that
my soul knoweth right well.
PSALM 139:14 KJV

I was born on:

In (city/state/country):

At:

I weighed in at _____pounds and _____ounces.

Everyone thought I resembled:

I have a unique birthmark and it looks like:

My parents' list of names for me included:

If they asked me, I would have named myself:

One story my parents tell me about the day I was born is:

Today I live in:

Back When I Was a Kid. . .

I walked seven miles a day to school. . .in the snow. . .barefoot.
And we didn't have TV or PlayStation. We had to shovel coal all day and play with rocks.

What I remember from age five is:

What I remember from age ten is:

Once I really hurt myself. The story is:

My favorite toys were:

My favorite childhood Christmas memories are:

My friend says:

What I remember from age five is:

What I remember from age ten is:

friends

when I was a kid

What scared me most as a child was:

What I worried about the most as a child was:

There is no room in love for fear. Well-formed love banishes fear. Since fear is crippling, a fearful life—fear of death, fear of judgment—is one not yet fully formed in love.

1 JOHN 4:18
THE MESSAGE

A few things I remember my parents made me do and I hated were:

A few things my parents made me eat that I hated were:

A few things I loved to eat as a child were:

Have a childhood sweetheart? ( ) Yes ( ) No Who? _____

What I remember about my childhood sweetheart is:

My Look

Be imitators of God, therefore, as dearly loved children and live a life of love,
just as Christ loved us and gave himself up for us as a fragrant offering and sacrifice to God.
EPHESIANS 5:1–2 NIV

If I were paid to write a character sketch of myself, this is what I might write:

This is the sketch I might draw:

If I had to compare myself to a movie star, I think I look like:

I'd rather look like:

If I could change one thing about my appearance, I'd change:

And the reason is:

I love who I am because:

My best quirks are:

this is who I am

- Why is it the stuff on the inside makes the outside truly beautiful?
- Why should a Christian's identity be grounded in God? (See 1 John 3:1.)
- Why are you so valuable to God—regardless of how you look?

My friend says:

I think appearance is:

Thoughts on my own appearance include:

One thing I want the owner of this book to know
about how they look is:

friends

this is who I am

> Though we travel the world over to
> find the beautiful, we must carry it
> with us or we will not find it.
> RALPH WALDO EMERSON

Thoughts on My Pad

"Take heed and beware of covetousness,
for one's life does not consist in the abundance of the things he possesses."
LUKE 12:15 NKJV

Where I live:

My house looks like:

Five great things about my room are:

Three things I'd like to change about my room are:

The thing in my room that most represents who I am is:

I am a (choose one) slob/clean fanatic.

If my house was on fire, the two things I would grab are:

My favorite things to do in the kitchen include:

Five things every bathroom must have (besides the hardware) are:

What I love about my backyard is:

The elements that I think make a house a home are:

What I feel about privacy is:

I've lived in _____ houses. Every time I move, I feel:

My craziest moving story is:

School Daze

The story on my school is:

Fave subjects:

Least fave subjects:

The teacher who taught me the most is:

What I learned from him/her was:

What I think is hardest about being a teacher is:

Fave things to do at school that have nothing to do with studying are:

school daze

Five things I wish were different
about my school are:

I long to accomplish
a great and noble task,
but it is my chief duty
to accomplish small
tasks as if they were
great and noble.
HELEN KELLER

My sports:

My clubs:

My activities:

My awards:

The most embarrassing moment in school for me was:

The best moment I can remember in school was:

My friend says:

The most embarrassing moment in school for me was:

The best moment I can remember in school was:

this is who I am

friends

My lunch box was:

My favorite school lunch was:

My favorite thing to do at recess as a kid was:

My locker contains:

The ideal locker contains:

If I ran the school, it'd be like this:

My friend says:

If I ran the school,
it'd be like this:

My favorite thing
to do at recess
as a kid was:

friends

Being Smart and Being Wise

For the LORD gives wisdom; from His mouth come knowledge and understanding.
PROVERBS 2:6 NKJV

I think being smart means:

I think the difference between smart and wise is:

From I Believe: The Way of Wisdom

- Disconnect from the world's lies and stand firmly in God's truth. "There is a way that seems right to a man, but in the end it leads to death" (Proverbs 14:12 NIV).

- Evaluate your weak points, then take action. "Let us throw off everything that hinders. . .and let us run with perseverance the race marked out for us" (Hebrews 12:1 NIV).

If I could have dinner with King Solomon, five things I'd ask him would be:

Three people I consider to be geniuses are:

My friend says:

The difference between smart and wise is:

friends

this is who I am

Heroes

I think a hero is:

I've seen heroes in action:

In everyone's life, at some time, our inner fire goes out. It is then burst into flame by an encounter with another human being. We should all be thankful for those people who rekindle the inner spirit.

ALBERT SCHWEITZER

From I Believe: How to Be a Hero

- Have compassion for others. Ask the Lord to show you how to be merciful, just as He is merciful.

- Reach out! Consider this: God reaches out to the unlovable, befriends those the world would rather forget, and touches those who seem untouchable.

- Set the standard. Living a double life is a surefire way to blow your witness—especially to a non-Christian. Remember, others are watching you.

The greatest lessons I have learned have been from:

My personal heroes have taught me:

Being Me

"Until now you have asked nothing in My name.
Ask, and you will receive, that your joy may be full."
JOHN 16:24 NKJV

What I like to do the most on a lazy day is:

Some of my favorite things in the world include:

The reason these things are my favorites is:

Favorites Buzz List

Favorite color:

Soda:

Junk food:

Restaurant for hanging with friends:

Restaurant to take a date:

Song:

Book:

Encouraging Bible verse:

Bible character:

Car:

Sport:

Superstar:

I am beginning to learn that it is the sweet, simple things of life which are the real ones after all.
LAURA INGALLS WILDER

this is who I am

Favorites Buzz List

Favorite color:

Soda:

Junk food:

Restaurant for hanging with friends:

Restaurant to take a date:

Song:

Book:

Encouraging Bible verse:

Bible character:

Car:

Sport:

Superstar:

friends

buzz list

Getting It All Out

Behold, I send you forth as sheep in the midst of wolves:
be ye therefore wise as serpents, and harmless as doves.
MATTHEW 10:16 KJV

Occasionally, we feel frustrated, angry, sad, or scared. The next couple of pages encourage you to spill in this book, but know throughout that God is listening to you when you talk with Him about your feelings. Family and the friends you trust are also there for you with love and support.

If I could go back and relive one year it would be:

What I hope would happen is:

How I feel about change is:

If I could change anything about my personality it would be:

I think my three worst traits are:

My friend says:

How I feel about change is:

If I could change anything about my personality it would be:

this is who I am

friends

page 25

Things that make me tongue-tied include:

Things I sometimes feel addicted to include:

Things that I find tempting include:

- Make a pact. Get your Christian friends together. Discuss things you've all struggled with as a result of peer pressure. Sign an agreement to hold each other accountable in these areas. Knowing others agree with you will help you stand firm when pressure sets in.

- Ask God for help. In your quiet times, ask God to remind you of your standards. Ask Him to strengthen you as He did the early disciples when they were faced with pressure to stop preaching the gospel.

The three things most likely to happen
when I lose my temper are:

It takes two to
make peace.
JOHN F. KENNEDY

Once I really lost my temper and the story is:

What I hate about being in a fight is:

The animal I'm most like when I'm angry is:

Things I tend to criticize are:

Criticisms that really bother me are:

this is who I am

What stresses me out is:

Therefore
humble yourselves
under the mighty hand
of God, that He may
exalt you at the proper
time, casting
all your anxiety on Him,
because He cares for you.
1 PETER 5:6–7 NASB

Five things I do to relieve stress are:

My phobias are:

When I'm anxious, the way you can tell is:

When I'm anxious, the best way to make me forget about it is:

My friend says:

What worries me is:

When I'm anxious, the way you can tell is:

f r i e n d s

this is who I am

I feel loneliest when:

Sometimes when I feel lonely, I:

You're blessed when you
feel you've lost what is
most dear to you.
Only then can you be
embraced by the One
most dear to you.
MATTHEW 5:4
THE MESSAGE

From I Believe: Handling Loneliness: Questions to Consider

- What's making me feel so lonely? Am I homesick? Am I anxious about something? Is some other unresolved issue at the root of my emotions?

- Am I not enough? Can't I find wholeness in the fact that I'm God's creation? Can't I still feel secure in my identity in Christ—even if that means being alone from time to time?

- What steps am I going to take to get through this loneliness?

- Do I feel lonely, anxious, or fearful more often than most people I know? Do I need professional help to work through these emotions?

What makes me cry is:

My scars are:

Good Vibrations

Laughter is the closest thing to the grace of God.
KARL BARTH

The funniest thing that has happened
in the last month is:

My friend says:

I laugh when:

Five things I think are truly funny are:

Five things I think
are truly funny are:

The things that get me really psyched are:

The things that
get me really
psyched are:

friends

If my friends were to describe me, I think they'd say:

At the mall, the first store I hit is:

When I get home from school, the first thing I do is:

If I have to run for food, the first place I'd go is:

In my downtime, I like to:

When I'm sick the only thing that makes me feel better is:

good vibrations

Five things I think are risky are:

You gain strength, courage, and confidence by every experience in which you really stop to look fear in the face. You are able to say to yourself, "I lived through this horror. I can take the next thing that comes along."
ELEANOR ROOSEVELT

The freakiest things I'd be willing to do are:

One time when I was literally very lost was:

I think courage is:

My friend says:

Five things I think are risky are:

The freakiest things I'd be willing to do are:

this is who I am

f r i e n d s

For we are His workmanship, created in Christ Jesus for good works,
which God prepared beforehand so that we would walk in them.

EPHESIANS 2:10 NASB

A story about one of my best days is:

A story about one of my worst days is:

Once, I pushed myself as far as I could go.
This is the story:

My proudest moment was:

good vibrations

this is who I am

Character Thoughts

Be strong and take heart,
all you who hope in the LORD.
PSALM 31:24 NIV

What makes a good character is:

My friend says:
What makes a
good character is:

What I think about being good is:

What I think about
being good is:

I think perseverance is:

What I think about
responsibility is:

What I think about responsibility is:

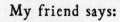

this is who I am

page 34

Celebrations

My favorite birthday party was:

My favorite birthday gift ever was:

If I could design my own birthday extravaganza,
it would look like this:

The worst birthday I ever had was:

One surprise party I had was:

I threw a surprise party once. The story is:

Holidays

My favorite holiday is:

My favorite foods at Thanksgiving are:

My favorite New Year's Eve memory is:

My favorite way to commemorate Easter is:

My best memories of July 4 include:

My friend says:

My favorite foods at Thanksgiving are:

My favorite way to commemorate Easter is:

Expressing Myself

Creations of my imagination include:

I'm crafty in the following ways:

If given a set of watercolors, I'd:

If given a pencil, I'd sketch:

Now he [Disney animator Matthew Luhn] works making movies, helping craft stories that harmonize with his convictions—getting toys safely across the freeway, getting kids safely through a theater. The story is king. And Luhn knows that kids who recognize a good story are prepared one day to hear an even better story, about an even more important rescue—about a King who knows them, loves them, and would seek them through all the seven seas.

FROM *THE CHRISTIAN READER*, JULY/AUGUST 2003

this is who I am

Man's mind stretched to a new idea
never goes back to its original dimensions.
OLIVER WENDELL HOLMES

If given an old typewriter, I'd write:

I like to dance to:

If participating in an extreme sport, my best event would be:

My friend says:

Creations of my imagination include:

I'm crafty in the following ways:

this is who they are:
family and friends

chapter two

The Family Vitals

Only a life lived for others is
a life worthwhile.
ALBERT EINSTEIN

My mom's full name is:

When and where she was born:

My dad's full name is:

When and where he was born:

I'm like my dad when I:

I'm like my mom when I:

Three things I would change about my parents are:

My favorite things about my mom are:

My favorite things about my dad are:

God sets the lonely
in families. . .
but the rebellious
live in a sun-
scorched land.
PSALM 68:6 NIV

The most memorable moment with my mom was:

The most memorable moment with my dad was:

My friend says:

The most memorable moment with my mom was:

The most memorable moment with my dad was:

this is who they are

page 40

friends

> A wise son accepts his father's discipline, but a scoffer does not listen to rebuke.
> PROVERBS 13:1 NASB

My mom's favorite saying is:

My dad's favorite saying is:

If I could pick two famous people to be my parents they would be:

Special things that my mom does for me are:

Everyday things I like to do with my mom include:

Special things that my dad does for me are:

Everyday things I like to do with my dad include:

this is who they are

> It is by his deeds that a lad distinguishes himself
> if his conduct is pure and right.
> PROVERBS 20:11 NASB

What I argue most with my parents about is:

Once I had a major blowout with my folks. The story is:

My parents discipline me by:

What I think about their discipline is:

> I have found that no kisses can ever compare to "mom" kisses, because mom kisses can heal anything. You can have a hangnail, a broken heart, or catatonic schizophrenia; with moms, one kiss and you're fine.
> ROBERT G. LEE

- Commit your life to the Lord, turn away from sin, and seek God for answers.
- Understand that no problem is too big for God to handle—not even a fight with Mom or Dad. God will set you on the right course if you let Him.
- Seek unity and solutions to problems, not strife and pointless quarrels.

My friend says:

Once I had a major blowout with my folks. The story is:

My parents discipline me by:

What I think about their discipline is:

Communicate: Share It E-mail:

What funny thing happened on your family vacation?

My family went on a month-long bike trip from our home in Ohio to Boston. Every night we would camp and sleep in tents. One night we forgot to take care of our dishes. In the middle of the night I woke up and heard my dad talking in the other tent. He thought he heard what he thought was a raccoon messing with our dishes, and so he started throwing rocks at the animal. It was a skunk!

SINGER4GOD

Family vacations we took included:

My favorite family vacation was:

On car trips, the games my family plays are:

On car trips, we always fight about:

What my parents did about the fighting was:

Post this at all the intersections, dear friends: Lead with your ears, follow up with your tongue, and let anger straggle along in the rear. God's righteousness doesn't grow from human anger.

JAMES 1:19
THE MESSAGE

My friend says:

My favorite family vacation was:

f r i e n d s

My Heritage

"Remember the days of long ago; think about the generations past. Ask your father and he will inform you."

DEUTERONOMY 32:7 NLT"

My ancestors come from:

One story of my heritage is:

Someday I hope to visit:

Every once in awhile you need to reflect on your family, especially your heritage. Like most people in America, you aren't that far removed from immigrant families who came to this country from another place. You may not be able to trace your ancestry to the Pilgrims, but you probably have some exciting and meaningful historical events in your family's past.

FROM *SIMPLE MATTERS* BY BRUCE AND STAN

this is who they are

My friend says:

One story of my heritage is:

friends

Siblings

My sibling[s] is/are:

The happiest moments of my life have been the few which I have passed at home in the bosom of my family.

THOMAS JEFFERSON

I'm most like my:

When we were little, we used to:

Our favorite family Christmas memory is:

siblings

Characteristics my sibling(s) have that I'd like to have are:

Communicate: Share It E-mail:

What is the funniest thing you did to your brother or sister and got away with?

I put vinegar and baking soda into a cup and said it was Sprite.

CHRISTY

Things that my sibling[s] do to drive me crazy are:

The things we used to fight about were:

One story about a fight we had is:

The funniest thing I ever did to my sibling and got away with was:

Three things I wish my sibling[s] knew about me are:

The Rest of the Family

My mom's father is:

My dad's father is:

My mom's mother is:

My dad's mother is:

My favorite memory of my mom's parents is:

My favorite memory of my dad's parents is:

When I visit my grandparents, the way they spoil me is:

The most memorable gift my grandparents ever gave me was:

The lessons I've learned from my grandparents include:

The simplest toy, one which even the youngest child can operate, is called a grandparent.
SAM LEVENSON

this is who they are

page 48

My favorite relative is _____because:

The story on my cousins is:

My favorite memories of my cousins include:

My favorite uncle is:

My favorite aunt is:

My favorite holiday traditions with our family include:

The reason relatives are better than friends is:

I wish I were (choose one) closer/not closer to my relatives because:

Five things I could do to get to know my relatives better are:

rest of the family

Friends

"Greater love has no one than this, that one lay down his life for his friends."
JOHN 15:13 NASB

My best friend in grade school was _____

My best friend in junior high was _____

My best friend in high school was _____

My favorite things to do with friends in grade school were:

Favorite things to do with friends in the summertime were:

When friends stayed over at my place, we liked to:

My favorite friend's place to stay over at when we were kids was:

It was the best because:

this is who they are

page 50

My friend[s] and I got into trouble as kids once. This is the story:

I met most of my friends doing:

The difference between my school friends and my church friends has been:

My friend says:

My favorite things to do with friends in grade school were:

My favorite things to do with friends in the summertime were:

friends

> Two are better than one, because they have a good return for their work:
> If one falls down, his friend can help him up.
> ECCLESIASTES 4:9–10 NIV

Traits I look for in a friend are:

A friend I can trust with my innermost secrets is:

Five traits that make me a good friend to others are:

Once a friend really stood up for me. The story is this:

A famous person I'd like as my friend is:

This is why:

- Take inventory of your friendships. Is popularity more important than genuine friendship? If your friends are leading you in the wrong direction and you continue to follow, beware: You're not living your life anymore—the crowd is.

- Sever bad ties—before you get tied up. When God says one thing in the Bible and your friends say another, then you must follow God and let your friends leave you if they wish. It's a hard choice but one Christians sometimes have to make.

- Seek Christian friends who share your values, and spend less time with friends who aren't interested in pursuing a godly walk. Like it or not, the people you spend time with have a big influence on your life.

One time, one of my friendships fell apart because:

A friend betrayed my trust by:

A time my friends asked me to do something that made me uncomfortable was when:

"Because a loveless world," said Jesus, "is a sightless world. If anyone loves me, he will carefully keep my word and my Father will love him—we'll move right into the neighborhood!"
JOHN 14:23
THE MESSAGE

this is who they are

Something a friend might do that I'd
consider almost unforgivable would be:

My friend says:
Something a friend might
do that I'd consider
almost unforgivable
would be:

If a friend betrayed my confidence,
I (choose one) would/wouldn't
forgive him or her.

The reason is:

If a friend betrayed my
confidence, I (choose
one) would/wouldn't
forgive him or her.

The reason is:

I lost a friend once. This is what happened.

Five ways to develop a new friendship are:

The best things about new friends are:

I like to make new friends by going to:

Once I tried making a new friend and she rejected me.
This what is happened and how I felt:

My friend says:

The best things about new friends are:

Once I tried making a new friend and she rejected me. This is what
happened and how I felt:

I I (choose one) would/wouldn't become friends with an unbeliever because:

This is what I share with unbelieving friends:

From I Believe: Be Real

- When you witness to an unbelieving friend, don't treat him or her like a project. Give others dignity and respect. Look at those different from you with Christ's compassionate eyes. Above all, check your motives. Ask yourself why you are sharing Christ at all. Is it to meet a church quota and to look spiritual—or is it out of real love and authentic faith? Being yourself is the best way for your friends to see the forces at work in your life.

This is how I share my faith with my friends:

For we are to God the aroma of Christ among those who are being saved and those who are perishing.
2 CORINTHIANS 2:15 NIV

I judge how someone is going to
be a good friend by:

What I think about popularity is:

What I would change about popularity and
unpopularity if I could would be:

A lot of us have a natural
tendency to evaluate peo-
ple before we decide we
want to care for them.
(Okay, we'll be honest—
we have a natural ten-
dency to do this, and it's
called judging.) Oh, we'll
be courteous and consid-
erate, but before we get to
the level of caring, we
qualify others first, as if
they have to meet some
kind of external standard.
By contrast, a caring person looks past the out-
ward dimension and gets
right to the heart. Rather
than prejudging people
before they even get to
know them, caring people
show genuine interest,
regardless of circum-
stances or personality.

FROM *SIMPLE MATTERS*
BY BRUCE AND STAN

friends

My friend who is most like me is:

The things we have in common are:

I see the difference of being a casual friend and a close friend as:

I wish I had more (choose one) casual/close friends.

The reason why is:

My two closest "guy" friends are:

My two closest "girl" friends are:

The difference between friends of opposite gender is:

this is who they are

♦ Why are other teens so cruel?. . .Why can't we speak words of kindness to each other? Every day the questions race through my brain.
You see, I'm a Christian in a school of unbelievers. . . .On top of that,
I'm a musician—not an athlete. In fact, I hate gym. I'm the teen who
is always picked last. Here's the crazy thing: At times, I've caught
myself thinking that I'm weird because I'm creative and not athletic.
What has saved me is the support I've gotten from my parents, my
church, and my youth group.

　An amazing thing is starting to happen. As I learn to accept
myself—and be confident in the person God made me to be—I'm
slowly gaining acceptance from others. . .even from some of the guys
who sometimes tease me. Above all, I'm striving to use words that
build up others. I'm treating people the way I want to be treated.

Ten things to do to treat others the way I want to be treated are:

My friend says:

Ten things to do to treat others the way I want to be treated are:

this is who they are

friends

Friendship Encouragers

Five things I like to do to encourage my friends are:

Times my friends are likely to need encouragement are when:

Ways I wish my friends would encourage me are:

My friends and I can encourage others by:

Reaching Out to Others

Three nice things I like to do for strangers are:

If I had a million dollars and had to give it away, I'd give it to:

If I had to tell a stranger one thing, I'd tell him or her:

From **I Believe:** A Can't-Miss Plan for Sharing Christian Love

- Accept the call to care. Think about modern-day outcasts: the glassy-eyed burnout at school or the geek who's always picked on in the halls. Would Jesus visit these people? Would He know their names, care about them, tell them stories? He would—and you should, too.

- Give a friend a love note. Write "I love you" in six different languages: "Je t' aime" (French), "Ti amo" (Italian), "Ai shite imasu" (Japanese), "Nagligivaget" (Eskimo), "Aloha wau ia oe" (Hawaiian), "S'agapo" (Greek).

> Do not withhold good from those to whom it is due, when it is in your power to do it.
> Do not say to your neighbor, "Go, and come back, and tomorrow I will give it."
>
> PROVERBS 3:27–28 NASB

If I had nothing but time to give, I'd like to:

My friend says:

Three nice things I like to do for strangers are:

The reason I tend not to reach out to strangers is:

If I had a million dollars and had to give it away, I'd give it to:

this is who they are

friends

reaching out

My Pet, My Friend

The godly are concerned for the welfare of their animals.
PROVERBS 12:10 NLT

Fur, fins, and feathers—some of our closest friends show us examples of the language of love and loyalty without ever uttering a word.

When I was younger, our pets were:

The silliest thing one of my pets ever did was:

I always wanted a_____but haven't owned one yet.

An exotic animal I'd love to have as a pet is:

A pet ran away once and I felt:

The greatest pleasure of a dog is that you may make a fool of yourself with him, and not only will he not scold you, but he will make a fool of himself, too.
SAMUEL BUTLER

Once I had a pet that died. I felt:

My friend says:

The silliest thing one of my pets ever did was:

Five things I've learned from my dog are:

An exotic animal I'd love to have as a pet is:

Five things I've learned from my cat are:

friends

Time spent with cats is never wasted.
COLETTE

this is what I think
about love, dating, and the opposite sex

chapter three

What Girls Think

I think the best thing about being a girl is:

Three things that I think drive girls crazy about guys are:

Three physical characteristics I think most girls look for in guys are:

Three personality traits I think most girls look for in guys are:

When a girl is upset with a guy, the first person I think she'd talk to about it is:

> Women are supposed to be very calm generally: but women feel just as men feel; they need exercise for their faculties, and a field for their efforts as much as their brothers do. . . . It is thoughtless to condemn them, or laugh at them, if they seek to do more or learn more than custom has pronounced necessary for their sex.
>
> CHARLOTTE BRONTË

> God created human beings; he created them godlike, reflecting God's nature.
> He created them male and female.
> GENESIS 1:27 THE MESSAGE

I feel that girls communicate by:

Ways I think guys show that they're interested are:

Ways I think guys show that they're not interested are:

I think the reason girls want to date is:

My friend says:

Three physical characteristics I think most girls look for in guys are:

Three personality traits I think most girls look for in guys are:

I feel that girls communicate by:

I think the reason girls want to date is:

friends

The reason girls decide to have sex is:

I think girls sometimes act very possessive because:

I think girls sometimes act very weird because:

Five ways for girls to avoid being weird are:

I think girls (choose one) act/don't act too much like guys these days.

What I think girls want guys to know about pornography is:

What Guys Think

Lord, when we are wrong, make us willing to change;
and when we are right, make us easy to live with.
PETER MARSHALL

I think the best thing about being a guy is:

Three things that I think drive guys crazy about girls are:

Ways I think guys show that they're interested are:

Ways I think guys show that they're not interested are:

Three physical characteristics I think most guys look for in girls are:

Three personality traits I think most guys look for in girls are:

this is what I think about...

O, what men dare do!
What men may do!
What men daily do,
not knowing what
they do!
WILLIAM SHAKESPEARE

I feel that guys communicate by:

I think the reason guys want to date is:

My friend says:

Three physical characteristics I think most guys look for in girls are:

Three personality traits I think most guys look for in girls are:

I feel that guys communicate by:

friends

what guys think

The reason guys choose to have sex is:

I think guys make dumb jokes because:

Five ways guys can avoid acting like goofballs are:

Five things guys want girls to know about how they act are:

Any man who says he can read a woman like a book is probably illiterate.
ANONYMOUS

Crushes

Kindergarten Crush_____

Third Grade Crush_____

Seventh Grade Crush _____

High School Crush _____

Prom Date_____

I know I have a crush on someone when I:

One secret crush I never told anyone about was:

One time I had a crush on a person and when I told him, he:

I met in the street
a very poor young
man who was in love.
His hat was old, his
coat threadbare—
there were holes
at his elbows; the
water passed through
his shoes and the stars
through his soul.
VICTOR HUGO

this is what I think about. . .

When I am rejected I feel:

If my best friend dated my crush I'd:

I can't believe I once had a crush on:

My famous person crushes include:

My weirdest crush was:

The most ridiculous thing I did when I had a crush was:

crushes

Flirting

"What I'm trying to do here is get you to relax, not be so preoccupied with *getting* so you can respond to God's *giving*. People who don't know God and the way he works fuss over these things, but you know both God and how he works. Steep yourself in God-reality, God-initiative, God-provisions. You'll find all your everyday human concerns will be met."

LUKE 12:29–31 THE MESSAGE

I think flirting is:

Three ways I flirt with a person are:

When someone flirts with me I feel:

My friend says:

Three ways I flirt with a person are:

One time I flirted with a stranger. Here's the story:

Flirting really bothers me when:

I think the good kind of flirting is:

Flirting really bothers me when:

this is what I think about. . . .

friends

I think the bad kind of flirting is:

One story of flirting gone bad is:

this is what I think about . . .

Six Big Differences Between Flirting and Sexual Harrassment

Some people confuse flirting with sexual harassment. They say or do something to another person, that person doesn't like it, and they think, "What's the big deal?" In fact, flirting and sexual harassment are very different.

▶ Flirting makes the other person feel good, happy, flattered, attractive, and in control. Sexual harassment makes the other person feel bad, angry, sad, demeaned, ugly, and powerless.

▶ Flirting can boost the other person's self-esteem. Sexual harassment hurts the other person's self-esteem.

▶ Flirting is reciprocal and complimentary. Sexual harassment is one-sided and degrading.

▶ Flirting is wanted and done among people who consider themselves equals. Sexual harassment is unwanted and done as a way for one person to have power over another.

▶ Flirting is legal. Sexual harassment is illegal. In schools, it's illegal according to Civil Rights Act Title IX of the Federal Education Amendments.

▶ Flirting is okay. Sexual harassment is not okay.

FROM *LIFE LISTS FOR TEENS*
BY PAMELA ESPELAND

Dating

My first date ever was:

My parents allowed me to date when:

I think the ideal age to start dating is:

My favorite date so far was:

I think you (choose one) should/shouldn't kiss on the first date.

The reason why is:

Three things I look for in a good date are:

My most embarrassing moment on a date was:

A famous person I would like to date is:

My famous person dream date would be:

My "regular person" dream date would be:

If I knew somebody liked me but wouldn't go out with me because of my age, I (choose one) would/would not lie about my age to go out with him or her.

What I think about dating a friend is:

My friend says:

A famous person I would like to date is:

My famous person dream date would be:

friends

I (choose one) think/don't think it's appropriate for a girl to ask out a guy.
The reason is:

What I think about girls paying for dates is:

Three cool places to meet and hang out with people are:

I would/would not go out on a blind date.
This is why:

I went on a blind date once. This is the story:

I feel that online dating is:

I met someone I liked online once. This is the story:

I feel that "speed" dating is:

dating

My definition for too much dating is:

I feel that exclusive dating is:

I feel that courtship is:

This important quality of a God-glorifying relationship is summed up in the Golden Rule:

"Do to others as you would have them do to you."
LUKE 6:31 NIV

We glorify God in our relationships when we put our needs aside and base our decisions on what serves the interests of the other person. We ask questions like these when we're guided by a selfless desire to do what's best for another:

- Is starting this relationship now what's best for her?

- Will expressing all my feelings now serve her?

- Are my actions encouraging her to love God more?

FROM *BOY MEETS GIRL*
BY JOSHUA HARRIS

. . . this is what I think about . . .

Dating Gone Wrong

Let your conversation be without covetousness; and be content with such things as ye have: for he hath said, I will never leave thee, nor forsake thee.
HEBREWS 13:5 KJV

Things that make me jealous are:

When I'm jealous I act:

What I think about cheating in a relationship:

Once I cheated on my significant other. This is the story:

My friend says:

When I'm jealous I act :

What I think about cheating in a relationship:

Once I cheated on my significant other.
This is the story:

this is what I think about. . .

Breakups

Heartbreak is life educating us.
GEORGE BERNARD SHAW

If the person I'm involved with cheated on me, I'd:

My worst breakup was:

My best breakup was:

The breakup I still have trouble talking about is:

The best way to recover from a breakup is:

breakups

Defining Love

My definition of love is:

The difference between love and attraction is:

I (choose one) have/have not been in love.

My first love's name was _____ and I was _____years old.

I (choose one) do/don't believe in love at first sight.
The reason why is:

One story I know about falling in love at first sight is:

My friend says:

The difference between love and attraction is:

I (choose one) do/don't believe in love at first sight.
The reason why is:

friends

A person who influenced me in a positive way on my beliefs on love was:

The reason why is:

A person who I'd never seek advice from on love or marriage is:

The reason why is:

Someone I loved once broke my heart and this is what I did to "get over" it:

What I would tell my parents if I thought I was in love:

Falling in love feels like:

I (choose one) will/won't avoid falling in love if there's a possibility I might get hurt.

The reason is:

What I think about commitment is:

I feel that love is (choose one) hard work/not hard work.
The reason why is:

Five best ways to show love are:

I think the key to staying in love is:

My friend says:

Five best ways to show love are:

I think the key to staying in love is:

friends

I think the way Hollywood portrays love is:

My favorite love song is:

Corniest pet name I've called the person I love is:

The corniest pet names ever are:

If my philosophy on love were packaged in a fortune cookie, it would read:

My friend says:

My favorite love song is:

Corniest pet name I've called the person I love is:

If my philosophy on love were packaged in a for-tune cookie, it would read:

friends

God's Plan for Love

> Love is patient, love is kind and is not jealous; love does not brag and is not arrogant, does not act unbecomingly; it does not seek its own, is not provoked, does not take into account a wrong suffered, does not rejoice in unrighteousness, but rejoices with the truth; bears all things, believes all things, hope all things, endures all things.
>
> 1 CORINTHIANS 13:4–7 NASB

Five characteristics that God states about love are:

From **I Believe:** How to Experience Supernatural Love

▶ Accept God's love. We've all heard that God loves us. And we know that God allowed His Son, Jesus Christ, to die on a cross and pay the penalty of our sin—which demonstrates the extent of His love. Then why don't we act as if this is the most incredible news we've ever heard? If God—the One who created us—says we are worthy of His love, why do we pursue what our culture thinks is cool in order to feel good about ourselves?

▶ Love as God loves. Need some ideas? Try this: Step out of your clique and get to know someone you normally wouldn't hang out with: the loner in the back of the class, the kid everyone picks on; pray with a hurting friend; send your parents on a date—and pay for it; volunteer to shovel snow from your neighbor's driveway.

Lust

To be "in lust" with someone means:

I know lust can cause:

Three things I saw this week that encouraged lust were:

My fears about lust are:

Three ways I work to keep my lust in check are:

For the grace of God that brings salvation has appeared to all men, teaching us that, denying ungodliness and worldly lusts, we should live soberly, righteously, and godly in the present age.

TITUS 2:11–12 NKJV

this is what I think about. . .

- Take a long, honest look at your sexuality. Then, accept the forgiveness of God and stop flogging yourself for your sexual failures. Persistent guilt and shame will make it difficult to shed sexual problems.

- Determine to change the way you think about the opposite sex. When you look at a guy or girl in sexual terms, "catch yourself" and train your mind to view others in nonsexual ways.

- Bring all your sexual thoughts and fantasies under conscious control by asking God to remind you when your thoughts need controlling.

- Acknowledge before God your lack of power to control your sexual urges, and pray that He will empower you to avoid temptation to sin by turning to healthy, wholesome activities.

- Keep in mind that sexual temptation is not sin. Some people are weakened by guilt from temptation. A pure mind is not a mind free of temptation. A pure mind chooses to act in the right way when temptation strikes.

- Steer clear of stuff that can feed your fantasies: movies, songs. . . steamy sites on the Internet.

- Watch what kind of friends you hang around with. Their language, habits, and humor will have an impact on you.

this is what I think about. . .

Sex

I think sex before marriage is:

I think purity means:

What my friends say about sex:

I have decided (choose one) to wait/to have sex.
This is why:

I think the relationship between sex and self-esteem are:

I know the consequences of having sex are:

And this is what I think of them:

What I'd do if I got pregnant/got someone pregnant:

God wants you to live a pure life. Keep yourselves from sexual promiscuity. Learn to appreciate and give dignity to your body, not abusing it, as is so common among those who know nothing of God.

1 THESSALONIANS 4:3–5
THE MESSAGE

this is what I think about. . . .

> You can lose your physical virginity just once. If you did it, you did it. You can't get that first time back again. And the past carries with it physical and emotional consequences. If memories have been etched on your brain, you can't pretend they're gone. But spiritually, it is quite possible to start all over again. Spiritual rebirth doesn't destroy the past. It transforms it. A second chance, spiritually, means there are no limitations to what you can become. The God who made the universe out of nothing can take your past and make from it something beautiful.
>
> FROM *CAMPUS LIFE*
> JANUARY/FEBRUARY 2001

I think sex with different partners affects my relationships in the future by:

My friend says:

I think sex with different partners affects my relationships in the future by:

My personal boundaries are:

My personal boundaries are:

Marriage

"For this reason a man will leave his father and mother
and be united to his wife, and the two will become one flesh."
EPHESIANS 5:31 NIV

I am (choose one) ready/not ready for marriage now because:

What I've learned from my parents' marriage is:

Five prerequisites before getting married are:

Everything that
touches us,
me and you,
takes us together
like a violin's bow,
which draws one
voice out of
two separate stings.
Upon what
instrument are we
two spanned?
And what musician
holds us in his hand?
RAINER MARIA RILKE

this is what fills my world

chapter four

Style

My style is:

My hairstyle is:

I think that contemporary clothing styles are:

My favorite designers are:

If I were a designer, my signature design would be:

Don't be concerned about the outward beauty that depends on fancy hairstyles, expensive jewelry, or beautiful clothes. You should be known for the beauty that comes from within, the unfading beauty of a gentle and quiet spirit, which is so precious to God.

1 PETER 3:3–4 NLT

If I lived in the fifties, my look might include:

If I lived in the sixties, my look might include:

If I lived in the seventies, my look might include:

If I lived in the eighties, my look might include:

The best places to shop are:

The weirdest item of clothing I own is:

If I were featured on a style disaster reality show, they would want to throw out:

And change my:

My friend says:

If I were featured on a style disaster reality show, they would want to throw out:

And change my:

f r i e n d s

Body and Soul

I think what makes a person beautiful is:

When I hear the phrase "beauty is in the eye of the beholder," I think:

What I think about makeup is:

What I think about plastic surgery is:

What I think about tattoos is:

If I ever decided to get a tattoo, it would be a:

And at age seventy, I think it will look:

What I think about body piercing is:

"The LORD does not look at the things man looks at. Man looks at the outward appearance, but the LORD looks at the heart."

1 SAMUEL 16:7 NIV

this is what fills my world

> Do you not know that your body is a temple of the Holy Spirit, who is in you, whom you have received from God? You are not your own; you were bought at a price. Therefore honor God with your body.
>
> 1 CORINTHIANS 6:19–20 NIV

When I see my body, I think:

What I think about weight loss is:

One story about obsessive body image I can tell is:

Three ways I know if someone has an eating disorder are:

Few people in my life would have any idea that I'm as consumed by my body as I am, but if I really look at my heart this is what I find. If I am honest with myself, I can see this is what lies beneath my well-adjusted, polished surface. From the outside I may look like a healthy, happy, young woman, but on the inside I know I often place more importance on my body than on my heart. I've allowed myself to believe the lie that my outward appearance determines my worth.

Something inside me tells me this is not how my life has to be. As the Holy Spirit stirs in my heart, God whispers to me to open the pages of my Bible. I try to ignore God's gentle prodding for other solutions.

FROM *CAMPUS LIFE*
SEPTEMBER/OCTOBER 2002

this is what fills my world

Advertising

Advertising that convinces me to buy things includes:

What I think about advertising is:

Five lies I know advertising sells to consumers are:

Three Ways to Fight Ad Creep

▶ Americans are drowning in advertising. The average American kid sees half a million commercials between birth and age eighteen. It's estimated that we see up to 3,000 advertisements a day. Refuse to be part of ad creep. How many logos are you wearing right now? Who's paying you to be a walking billboard?

▶ The next time you go shopping for a basic—like a black T-shirt—find one with your favorite logo. Then find one with no logo. Compare prices. Do you really want to pay for the privilege of advertising a company's products?

▶ Tired of ads before movies, at the ATM, on your computer, on the sidewalks, on lampposts, on blimps, on buses, in the bathroom at your favorite restaurant? If you are, complain. Write to the advertisers and tell them what you think. Visit the BadAds Web site (www.badads.com) for tons of ideas and helpful links.

ADAPTED FROM *LIFE LISTS FOR TEENS* BY PAMELA ESPELAND

Hollywood

The celebrity I'd most like to meet is:

A celebrity I can't stand is:

The celebrity I'd most like to pull a prank on is:

A celebrity who I think is totally fake is:

Celebrities who I think actually use their influence for good are:

The child celebrity I hope has a career comeback is:

A celebrity is a person who works hard all his life to become well known, then wears dark glasses to avoid being recognized.
FRED ALLEN

My friend says:

The celebrity I'd most like to meet is:

A celebrity I can't stand is:

The celebrity I'd most like to pull a prank on is:

A celebrity who I think is totally fake is:

Celebrities who I think actually use their influence for good are:

The child celebrity I hope has a career comeback is:

friends

> Be imitators of God, therefore, as dearly loved children and live a life of love,
> just as Christ loved us and gave himself up for us as a fragrant offering and sacrifice to God.
> EPHESIANS 5:1–2 NIV

If I were a celebrity, I'd:

In truth, how I feel about celebrity gossip is:

The celebrity who I think gets too much press is:

If I were part of the paparazzi, I would want to follow:

The award show I'd most want to attend is:

A personal friend who I think will someday be a celebrity is:

hollywood

this is what fills my world

Movies

I go to the movies because:

I spend _____ hours at the movies a month.

My favorite person to go to the movies with is:

My favorite movies are:

If I could direct a movie, I'd want to direct:

Movies that inspire me to be a better person include:

Movies that I think are very funny include:

What I think of the way movies portray romance is:

What I think of the way movies
portray violence is:

I believe violence (choose one) does/doesn't
desensitize you because:

The first horror movie I ever saw was:

It affected me in this way:

What I think about horror movies is:

From Scripture, we know
that God's power is greater than
Satan's (1 John 4:4).
We have an advantage in our
battles with evil that heroes in
horror movies don't: strength
and support from God.

Here are some other things
I try to think about, too:

How is the murder of
humans—whether good guys
or bad guys—treated?

When violence is used, is
it glorified, or used just for
effect? Is it presented in a way
that is supposed to thrill
or shock the viewer?

Are demons, magic, and
other supernatural elements
used as plot devices, or are
they metaphors meant to
communicate something
about good and evil?

What is biblically true here?
What is false?

How would I change this
to become more true to my
understanding of God and
what He tells us about evil?

FROM *CAMPUS LIFE*
SEPTEMBER/OCTOBER 2003

this is what fills my world

Television

I like to watch:

What I think is trashy about television is:

If I had my own television network, my programming would be:

What I think about reality television is:

If I participated in a reality show, it'd be:

The reason is:

My friend says:

What I think about reality television is:

If I participated in a reality show, it'd be:

Music

Music is the art of the prophets, the only art that can calm the agitations of the soul;
it is one of the most magnificent and delightful present God has given us.

MARTIN LUTHER

My favorite music artist is:

My favorite CDs are:

My favorite lyrics are:

My best concert experience was:

I think really good music should:

What I think about negative lyrics is:

My friend says:

My favorite CDs are:

My best concert
experience was:

friends

I spend $ _____ on CDs every year.

I (choose one) download/don't download
music off the web.

What I think about downloading music online is:

God holds me head and
shoulders above all who
try to pull me down.
I'm headed for his place
to offer anthems that
will raise the roof!
Already I'm singing
God-songs; I'm
making music to God.
PSALM 27:6
THE MESSAGE

If I produced a music video, it'd be:

I (choose one) watch/don't watch music and video awards shows.

I think music artists are:

If I were a rock star, I'd be most like:

Books

List of my favorite books and authors:

Three books I had to read for school that I hated were:

My favorite characters from books are:

If I wrote a best-selling novel, it would be about:

I think reading is (choose one) good/bad because:

My favorite place to buy books is:

Because for some of us, books are as important as almost anything else on earth. What a miracle it is that out of these small, flat, rigid squares of paper unfolds world after world after world, worlds that sing to you, comfort and quiet or excite you. Books help us understand who we are and how we are to behave. They show us what community and friendship mean; they show us how to live and die. . . . An author makes you notice, makes you pay attention, and this is a great gift. My gratitude for good writing is unbounded; I'm grateful for it the way I'm grateful for the ocean. Aren't you? I ask.

FROM *BIRD BY BIRD* BY ANNE LAMOTT

Magazines

My favorite magazines are:

My favorite sections to read in magazines are:

The pictures in magazines make me feel:

My favorite magazine stories are about:

The celebrity gossip in magazines makes me think:

If I were a magazine editor, I'd create a magazine called:

It'd look like this:

My friend says:

If I were a magazine editor, I'd create a magazine called:

It'd look like this:

friends

Video Games

I spend _____ hours a week playing video games.

My game system is:

My favorite types of video games are:

My favorite games are:

The game character I'm most like is:

Because:

I think violence in video games is:

If I designed a video game, it would be about:

My friend says:

My favorite games are:

If I designed a video game it would be about:

f r i e n d s

Are you gaming wisely?

1. Pray about your choice. I'm serious here! God will help you with every decision you face—big or small. James 1:5 promises, "If any of you lacks wisdom, he should ask God, who gives generously to all without finding fault, and it will be given to him" (NIV).

2. Talk to Mom and Dad. Once they regain consciousness, they'll come through with some great advice. Bottom line: Your parents call the shots in your life. It's up to you to honor them.

3. Ask yourself two key questions. Will the game require you to be the kind of hero who reflects godly character? Or is it leading you to make poor moral choices in the name of fantasy?

4. Uncover the "hidden agendas." Just about every game promotes some kind of belief or philosophy. Here are two common ones to identify and avoid:

Violent problem solving: "Wipe out people and property to score points. Crush! Kill! Destroy! And you'll be rewarded for it!" In other words, you put your faith in firepower.

The Occult: "Rely on dark supernatural powers; cast spells and use sorcery to be victorious." Games with occult themes toy with demonic activity, twist truth, and often place humans on the same level with God.

The best kinds of games to play are those that promote healthy competition and good sportsmanship—even the kind in which truth and justice triumph over evil.

FROM *BREAKAWAY*
JANUARY 2002

Going Online

I spend _____ hours a day online.

My favorites things to do online are:

My favorite sites to visit are:

Five great things about the Internet are:

Five things I'd change about the Internet are:

What I (choose one) like/don't like
about e-mail is:

My friend says:

My favorites things to do
online are:

My favorite sites
to visit are:

f r i e n d s

this is what fills my world

Two things to consider when surfing:

▸ SURF IN PUBLIC. Forty-three percent of you [*Campus Life* readers] surf the Net in the family room, living room, or den. That's good. Surfing in a "public" place, where other family members can see you, makes you think twice about visiting certain Web sites or chatting with the wrong people. Twenty-three percent of you surf the Web in your bedrooms. That kind of privacy is a recipe for online danger. Our advice: Use your bedroom computer as a word processor and for playing computer games, but disconnect it from the Net. Use the "public" one for surfing, and only when other people are around. Cyberstalkers are less likely to try to contact you if they know your parents could be reading it.

▸ WWJD? Though it's become almost a cliché, it's a good question to keep in mind whenever you're online: What would Jesus do? Ask God to help you be wise while you're on the Net. As a constant reminder, cut out the verse [above] and tape it to your monitor.

FROM *CAMPUS LIFE*
NOVEMBER/DECEMBER 2000

Whatever is true, whatever is noble, whatever is right, whatever is pure, whatever is lovely, whatever is admirable—if anything is excellent or praiseworthy—think about such things.
PHILIPPIANS 4:8 NIV

I shop online for:

My favorite sites to shop from are:

What I like to chat about is:

One time I chatted with a stranger, and the story is:

I think you (choose one) should/shouldn't meet people in person whom you've met online.

Money, Cash, Dough, Green

My doctor said I look like a million dollars—green and wrinkled.
RED SKELTON

My allowance as a child was:

My allowance now is:

The way I earn money is:

What I think money is good for is:

I'd like to have a million dollars because:

I have a credit card and I use it to:

I'm learning financial responsibility by:

My friend says:

I'd like to have a million dollars because:

I'm learning financial responsibility by:

friends

What I think about tithing is:

One time money (or the lack of it) got me into trouble, and the story is:

money, cash

Once I saw real poverty. This is what it looked like:

I have a savings account and it's for:

> Whoever loves money never has money enough; whoever loves wealth is never satisfied with his income. This too is meaningless.
>
> ECCLESIASTES 5:10 NIV

Addictions

For in that He Himself has suffered, being tempted, He is able to aid those who are tempted.
HEBREWS 2:18 NKJV

I think smoking is:

How I feel about the pressure to smoke or drink is:

I think drinking is:

I think people get drunk because:

I knew someone who drove drunk once. This is the story:

From I Believe: How to Choose Wisely

- The fact is, you—and only you—are responsible for your actions. Making the right choices, and dealing with the wrong ones, is something you'll have to shoulder all by yourself.

- Will you choose to bend the rules from time to time (knowing that you can), or will you commit to an unshakable faith in Christ? *Now* is the time to decide. Like it or not, the days ahead will be filled with all kinds of temptations.

this is what fills my world

I think that doing drugs is:

I think people get high because:

My friend says:

I think drinking is:

I think that doing drugs is:

f r i e n d s

As I listen to Jeremy, I'm struck by something: Here's a guy who was just experimenting with alcohol and cigarettes. He gave in to that little voice in his head saying, Try it. It's cool! That mistake led to another, and another. He lost friends, he betrayed his parents, and he fell away from God because he didn't turn down that first drink.

So what did it take for Jeremy to reach out for help? "There were a lot of things that made me think about what I was doing to myself," Jeremy says. "There was that time I stopped my car on the highway. There was the time I was drinking with an old girlfriend and she ended up forcing me to have sex with her. There was the time I blew my nose after snorting coke and chunks of flesh came out.

"But if I had to pinpoint something that really made me want to change, it was getting to college and being around all these Christians. That's why I wanted to be at a Christian college. I'd pretty much forgotten about God by that point, but I thought it would be a place I could escape from all the drugs."

FROM *CAMPUS LIFE*
JULY/AUGUST 1998

Language

Do not let any unwholesome talk come out of your mouths, but only what is helpful for building others up according to their needs, that it may benefit those who listen. . . . Nor should there be obscenity, foolish talk or coarse joking, which are out of place, but rather thanksgiving.

EPHESIANS 4:29; 5:4 NIV

Once, when my parents caught me cursing, they:

I think that cursing is:

I think that "replacement words" for cursing are:

The curses I'm most likely to use are:

When someone curses at me I feel like:

My friend says:

I think that cursing is:

The curses I'm most likely to use are:

friends

this is what fills my world

War

I think that war is:

For unto us a Child is born, unto us a Son is given; and the government will be upon His shoulder. And His name will be called Wonderful, Counselor, Mighty God, Everlasting Father, Prince of Peace.

ISAIAH 9:6 NKJV

I think that a mandatory draft is:

Ideals that I believe fighting for include:

One thing I'd tell government officials about war if I could is:

A family member/friend has been to war and one story they told me was:

this is what I believe

chapter five

Thoughts about God

This is what I think about God:

Yet he. . .gave glory to God,
being fully persuaded that
God had power to do what
he had promised.
ROMANS 4:20–21 NIV

When I imagine God, He looks like:

Why I think God created us:

Five questions I'd like to ask God are:

What I think of when I call God "Father":

My friend says:

This is what I think about God:

Five questions I'd like to ask God are:

Why I think God created us:

From **I Believe:** God Is Personal—The God Who Comforts

- God loves us, and He reaches out to us on a very personal level (Matthew 7:21).
- God is interactive (Matthew 6:10).
- God speaks and listens (Genesis 1:3; Psalm 94:9).
- God feels (Genesis 6:6; Deuteronomy 1:37; Exodus 20:5; Psalm 111:4).
- God has a name—He isn't just an "it" (Genesis 4:26; Exodus 20:7; Exodus 20:24; Exodus 23:21; Ezekiel 43:7-8).
- God created us (Acts 17:24, Ephesians 1:11).

I think holiness is:

I believe the Holy Spirit is real because:

I believe things happen by (choose one) chance/my life predestined by God.

What I think of the question "Why does God allow bad things to happen?"

thoughts about God

this is what I believe

Jesus

I accepted Jesus into my life at age:

And this is what happened:

I believe Jesus is the Son of God because:

As a boy, I think Jesus was like:

As a man, I think Jesus was like:

this is what I believe

Because the God of the Bible is a triune God—Father, Son, and Holy Spirit—I picture Jesus as the person of God who is talking, listening, encouraging, correcting, and spending time with me. When I see Jesus as the actual Person, I am communicating with a Person. And though His physical appearance and apparel might lack detail, the mental picture that I have of Him is of a gentle shepherd, a hardworking carpenter, a teacher, and a man who liked to fish with His friends. By referring to the image of Jesus as a shepherd, carpenter, teacher, or fisherman, I am extremely comfortable and never threatened during my hour appointment with Him. In those minutes, I am freely communicating with a kind, gentle, powerful friend, and Father rather than a kingly, unapproachable ruler.

FROM *LET FAITH CHANGE YOUR LIFE* BY BECKY TIRABASSI

The traits of Jesus I'd like to reflect the most in my life are:

"But so that you may know that the Son of Man has authority on earth to forgive sins"—then He said to the paralytic—"Get up, pick up your bed and go home." And he got up and went home.

MATTHEW 9:6–7 NASB

The most important things I think Jesus taught were:

The miracle I would've most liked to see Jesus perform was:

I believe the resurrection of Jesus is true because:

If I could have dinner with Jesus, I'd ask Him:

My friend says:

The most important things I think Jesus taught were:

f r i e n d s

this is what I believe

The Bible

For the word of God is living and active. Sharper than any double-edged sword,
it penetrates even to dividing soul and spirit, joints and marrow;
it judges the thoughts and attitudes of the heart.

HEBREWS 4:12 NIV

What I think about the Bible is:

A Bible story that has greatly influenced my life is:

When I'm having a bad day, I read this verse to encourage myself:

This is how often I read the Bible:

The Bible verse that is most meaningful in my life is:

This is how I feel about the Bible's relevance to my daily life:

this is what I believe

Things I don't understand in the Bible include:

If I could, I'd ask Adam and Eve:

If I could, I'd ask Moses:

If I could, I'd ask King David:

If I could, I'd ask Job:

If I could, I'd ask Mary:

If I could, I'd ask Peter:

If I could, I'd ask Paul:

My friend says:

The Bible verse that is most meaningful in my life is:

friends

Up until the age of twenty-one, I considered the Bible to be a token leather book one receives upon completing confirmation classes! I changed my mind about that leather book when I became desperate enough to search for, look for, even grasp for something or someone outside myself to change and help me. It was only then that I understood that the Bible was God's Word, and if I wanted to get to know God better, I'd need to read.

FROM *LET FAITH CHANGE YOUR LIFE* BY BECKY TIRABASSI

this is what I believe

Prayer

The prayers I learned as a child were:

Things I pray for include now:

My favorite way to talk to God is:

One prayer God answered that changed my world was:

A prayer that hasn't been answered yet is:

I never went to bed in my life and I never ate a meal in my life without saying a prayer. I know my prayers have been answered thousands of times, and I know that I never said a prayer in my life without something good coming of it.

JACK DEMPSEY

Do not have your concert first and tune your instruments afterwards.
Begin the day with God.

HUDSON TAYLOR

this is what I believe

Faith

I define faith as:

Sometimes I have doubts because:

My faith is weak when:

My faith grows strong when I:

I know God is faithful because:

From **I Believe:** Be Faithful—Just as God Is Faithful

When people look at your life, make sure they see. . .

. . .someone constantly dying to Jesus.

. . .a person of integrity who dares to put his or her life on the line for the gospel.

. . .a teen with a sincere heart—not a guy or girl hiding behind a mask.

Truth

What is the truth?

The biggest lie I've ever told was:

I think most people (choose one) tell the truth/lie.

I believe there is so much lying in the world because:

One time I got caught lying and this is what happened:

- Desire truth. While most Christian teens understand that their lives could—and *should*—be a reflection of Jesus Christ, they allow peer fear to get in the way. Jesus said, "Then you will know the truth, and the truth will set you free" (John 8:32 NIV). Are you among the many who haven't allowed the truth to set them free? If so, it's time for a change.

- Choose truth. If you're ready to allow God to speak words of truth to you, it's time to do something radical. Sit down in the quietness of your room (no stereo, please), and let the invisible God speak the truth to you through His Word. The Bible isn't only for parents and pastors; it's for *you!* The only way you can believe the truth is to know the truth.

Confession

What I think it means to confess your sins is:

Why I think it is hard for us to confess things we've done wrong is:

What I think it means to be broken is:

One time I confessed a wrongdoing to a friend/family member.
This is the story:

It can be hard to ask for forgiveness because:

> To be alive is to be broken. And to be broken is to stand in need of grace. Honesty keeps us in touch with our neediness and the truth that we are saved sinners. There is a beautiful transparency to honest disciples who never wear a false face and do not pretend to be anything but who they are.
>
> FROM *THE RAGAMUFFIN GOSPEL* BY BRENNAN MANNING

My friend says:

Why I think it is hard for us to confess things we've done wrong is:

One time I confessed a wrongdoing to a friend/family member.
This is the story:

friends

Forgiveness and Grace

Forgiveness is important because:

A person I have a hard time forgiving is:

One story of a friend/family member forgiving me is:

I believe grace is:

The Good News means we can stop lying to ourselves. The sweet sound of amazing grace saves us from the necessity of self-deception. It keeps us from denying that though Christ was victorious, the battle with lust, greed, and pride still rages within us. As a sinner who has been redeemed, I can acknowledge that I am often unloving, irritable, angry, and resentful with those closest to me. When I go to church I can leave my white hat at home and admit I have failed. God not only loves me as I am, but knows me as I am.

FROM *THE RAGAMUFFIN GOSPEL* BY BRENNAN MANNING

I think the difference between "doing stuff to be a Christian" and "being a Christian" is:

I can show grace to others by:

Gratitude

Things that I'm thankful for are:

Things I probably take for granted are:

The importance of an "attitude of gratitude" is:

The best ways I think to show thankfulness are:

Get down on your knees and thank God you are on your feet.
IRISH SAYING

this is what I believe

My friend says:

Things that I'm thankful for are:

friends

Sharing Christ

I am not ashamed of the gospel, because it is the power of God for the salvation of everyone who believes: first for the Jew, then for the Gentile.

ROMANS 1:16 NIV

This is how I communicate Christ to others:

What I think it means to be "salt and light" is:

Before I share my faith, I feel:

Reasons I don't share my faith include:

If I could share the message of Christ to one unbelieving person and be certain he or she would accept Jesus, the person would be:

One thing I would tell a non-Christian would be:

There are two ways of spreading light: to be the candle or the mirror that reflects it.

EDITH WHARTON

this is what I believe

From **Communicate:**

Knowing what to say and do without looking like a wishy-washy Christian geek isn't easy. What's the answer? Here are a few ideas on how to keep firm when your knees are weak:

1. Rehearse. With a parent, friend, or youth leader, go through as many situations you can think of that could cause you to do the wrong thing when a dilemma hits. If you know what to expect and what to say— before it happens—you'll be much more confident.

2. Get the word out. Unfortunately, many Christians want to be full-time in God's Secret Service and hide their faith. But you don't have to hand out tracts with your testimony on them to inform your co-workers of your allegiance to Christ. Instead, drop a few signals:

Ask questions: "Does your family have any Christmas (Easter) traditions? We go to church on Christmas Eve and. . ."

Read a pocket Bible or a Christian book on your break.

When someone mentions a struggle they're going through, let them know you'll pray for them. How? A short note or quick word is often all it takes.

3. Let your actions speak loudly. Your tasks at work come first. If you're not a good employee, you may end up giving all Christians a bad name.

4. Hold your tongue. When other workers start telling off-color jokes or making crude remarks, fight the urge to participate. Don't act superior or judgmental (after all, non-Christians will act like non-Christians); just try to keep quiet or turn away. Yes, it may mean it will take longer to be included in the group, but in the long run, what type of reputation do you want—a sheep who'll blend in with the gang because it's safe, or a person of character who has a firm moral foundation?

Community

I think being a Christian means:

What I appreciate most about fellow believers is:

I feel I can depend on fellow believers for:

Five things I wish most Christians (including myself) would do better:

Five ways I can make a change in people's lives every day are:

My friend says:

Five ways I can make a change in people's lives every day are:

Courage is contagious. When a brave man takes a stand, the spines of others are often stiffened.
BILLY GRAHAM

I (choose one) would/wouldn't share Christ if it meant putting myself into danger.

Ways I get involved with my Christian community include:

I'd like to take a mission trip to:

Once I went on a mission trip. This is the story:

Go, therefore, and make disciples of all nations, baptizing them in the name of the Father and of the Son and of the Holy Spirit, teaching them to observe everything I have commanded you. And remember, I am with you always, to the end of the age.
MATTHEW 28:19–20 HCSB

this is what I believe

Church Life

And He Himself gave some to be apostles, some prophets, some evangelists, and some pastors and teachers, for the equipping of the saints for the work of ministry, for the edifying of the body of Christ, till we all come to the unity of the faith and of the knowledge of the Son of God, to a perfect man, to the measure of the stature of the fullness of Christ.

EPHESIANS 4:11–13 NKJV

My first church experience that I remember was:

My church background is:

What I thought about going to church then was:

What I think about church now is:

Memories from Sunday school include:

Memories from Vacation Bible School include:

Memories from church camp include:

What I love about worship is:

What I'd change about the way I worship is:

Favorite hymn:

Favorite chorus:

Favorite topic to hear someone speak on:

If I were a pastor, I'd:

church life

Favorite things I do with my youth group are:

My friend says:

My church background is:

f r i e n d s

What I think about church now is:

My youth (or discipleship) group is important to me because:

It took me a while to understand that the answer to problems was not marketing or programs but rather spirituality. If we needed to reach youth, we wouldn't do a pizza feed and game night, we would get together and pray and fast and ask God what to do. God led some guys to start a homeless teen outreach downtown, and now they feed about one hundred homeless teenagers every week. It is the nuttiest youth group you will ever see, but that's what God said to do. I love that sort of thing because rather than the church serving itself, the church is serving the lost and the lonely. It gives me chills when I think about it because it is that beautiful of a thing.

FROM *BLUE LIKE JAZZ*
BY DONALD MILLER

Church and State

What I think about prayer in public schools is:

What I think about the Ten Commandments or other Bible verses
in government buildings is:

What I think about legal abortions is:

I feel that Christians in public office should:

From **I Believe:** Know Your Rights

The Constitutions of both the United States and Canada protect your freedom
of religious expression. Do you know what you can do on a public school campus?

- Students can pray on a public school campus.
- Students can read their Bibles on a public school campus.
- Students can form religious clubs on campus if other extracurricular clubs exist.
- Students can hand out tracts, flyers, or other religious materials on campus.
- Students can do research papers, speeches, and so forth, with religious themes.
- Students can be exempt from participating in assignments that are contrary to their religious beliefs.
- Students can discuss religious issues although other students may hear them.

Mysteries of Life

Miracles, in the sense of phenomena we cannot explain,
surround us on every hand: Life itself is the miracle of miracles.
GEORGE BERNARD SHAW

Once I met a stranger and I'm certain he/she was an angel.
This is the story:

What I think about life on other planets is:

When people talk about evolution, my response is:

The biggest question I have about science is:

What I think about the origin of the world is:

The coolest thing about natural mysteries is:

Heaven

This is what I think happens when we die:

I lost someone I loved once. This is the story:

We all long for heaven where God is, but we have it in our power to be in heaven with Him right now—to be happy with Him at this very moment. But being happy with Him now means loving like He loves, helping like He helps, giving as He gives, serving as He serves, rescuing as He rescues, being with Him twenty-four hours a day—touching Him in His distressing disguise.

FROM *MOTHER TERESA: CONTEMPLATIVE IN THE HEART OF THE WORLD*, BY ANGELO DeVANANDA

I'm looking forward to meeting _____ in heaven.

This is what I think heaven looks like:

"In my Father's house are many rooms; if it were not so, I would have told you.
I am going there to prepare a place for you."
JOHN 14:2 NIV

What will be heaven to me is:

Five ways to live a little heaven on earth today are:

My friend says:

This is what I think happens when we die:

This is what I think heaven looks like:

What will be heaven to me is:

Five ways to live a little heaven on earth today are:

friends

Thoughts from Psalms and Proverbs

What's a psalm? When King David wrote the book of Psalms, very simply put, it was a collection of his greatest song lyrics. David was a poet and songwriter, a shepherd and a king, and the psalms reflect his journey with God. Some are cries for help, others are prayers for forgiveness and mercy, and many are praises and thanks. They contain an abundance of rich examples of someone passionate about a personal relationship with a loving Creator.

My favorite Psalm is:

Because:

In the Psalms, what I learn about David is:

In the Psalms, what I learn about God is:

If I wrote a psalm, this is what it'd be:

> The LORD is my rock, my fortress and my deliverer; my God is my rock, in whom I take refuge. He is my shield and the horn of my salvation, my stronghold.
> PSALM 18:2 NIV

What's a proverb?

A proverb is defined as a short, wise saying, embodying some important fact of experience and generally taken as truth. King Solomon wrote an entire book full of proverbs in the Bible—and that's the origin of the word, from the book of Proverbs.

Common proverbs include phrases like, "Beauty is only skin deep" and "An honest answer is like a kiss on the lips."

For through me your days will be many, and years will be added to your life.
PROVERBS 9:11 NIV

Other common proverbs relevant to my life are:

Five of my own proverbs that I think should be practiced in everyday life are:

My friend says:

If I wrote a psalm, this is what it'd be:

friends

this is who I want to be

Dreaming and Becoming

Hitch your wagon
to a star.
RALPH WALDO
EMERSON

What I wanted to be at

Age five:

Age ten:

Age fifteen:

What my dreams are now:

A person who encourages my dreams is:

Forgetting what is behind
and straining toward what
is ahead, I press on toward
the goal to win the prize
for which God has called me
heavenward in Christ Jesus.
PHILIPPIANS 3:13–14 NIV

Five places I'd like to live someday are:

If I could change places with one person for a day, I'd trade places with:

The reason is:

If I could do anything in the world, it would be:

My dream house looks like:

My dream vacations are:

The role I believe God plays in my dreams is:

Nevertheless I am continually with You; You hold me by my right hand. You will guide me with Your counsel, and afterward receive me to glory.

PSALM 73:23–24 NKJV

Education Plans

If I were asked to speak at my graduation, what I'd say is:

What I'd like to do after graduating high school is:

I might go to college at:

At college I might major in:

In college, the activities I'd like to be involved in are:

While in college, I'd like to live:

this is who I want to be

Five elements that I think make for a good
college experience are:

Fall seven times,
stand up eight.
JAPANESE
PROVERB

I'd like to do an internship at:

My friend says:

What I'd like to do after
graduating high school is:

I might go to college at:

I might go to grad school and study:

At college I might
major in:

this is who I want to be

friends

Work

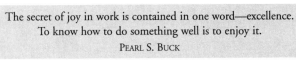

> The secret of joy in work is contained in one word—excellence.
> To know how to do something well is to enjoy it.
> PEARL S. BUCK

My first job ever was:

My current job is:

My favorite job so far has been:

What I've learned on the job is:

If I became president, I'd:

If I became king/queen of a small country, I'd:

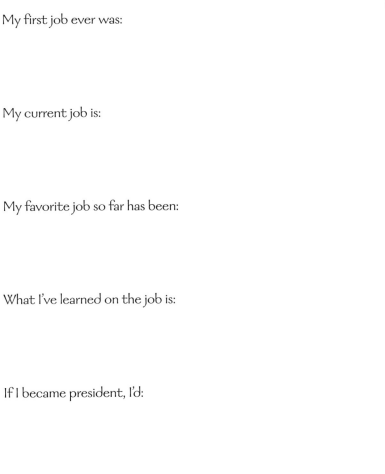

One outside job I'd love to have is:

One desk job I'd love to have is:

Three jobs that I know I'd hate are:

Three jobs that I know I'd love are:

If I owned my own business, it would be:

work

My friend says:

Three jobs that I know I'd love are:

If I owned my own business, it would be:

friends

Goals

"For I know the plans I have for you," declares the LORD,
"plans to prosper you and not to harm you, plans to give you hope and a future."
JEREMIAH 29:11 NIV

What I think success is:

What I think about failure is:

Major goals I have already achieved are:

Three goals for the next year are:

I prioritize by:

I think my life priorities should be:

My friend says:

Major goals I have
already achieved are:

I think my life
priorities should be:

friends

this is who I want to be

Two emotionally related goals are:

Two physically related goals are:

Two spiritually related goals are:

What I want people to think about me while I'm alive is:

In the corporate world, companies adopt a "mission statement" to articulate what is important to them. The mission statement states the core values by which the company operates. A personal mission statement is like a personal constitution. Like the U.S. Constitution, your personal mission statement should be timeless (stating your personal philosophy and beliefs that apply to your life at any age) and idealistic (stating the standard to which you aspire, even though you fall short sometimes).

FROM *GOD IS IN THE SMALL STUFF (AND IT ALL MATTERS)* BY BRUCE AND STAN

What I want people to say about me when I'm gone is:

My personal mission statement is:

this is who I want to be

Three ways I can be accountable for working toward my goals are:

There are some things one can only achieve by a deliberate leap in the opposite direction.
FRANZ KAFKA

Five crazy things that no one knows I want to do are:

Five things I want to do in the next ten years are:

From I Believe: A Road Map to Success

- Ask yourself this question: "Is the Lord directing my steps?" If so, Proverbs 16:3 promises that you're on the right track: "Commit to the Lord whatever you do, and your plans will succeed" (NIV). But keep in mind that your plans have no strength if they're not from God.

- Pursue what is kind, just, and loving in life: "Better a little with righteousness than much gain with injustice" (Proverbs 16:8 NIV).

- Be still and listen. Get away regularly and have a personal retreat. Find a quiet place where you can focus on His voice and direction for your life.

- Map out what you sense God is telling you. Putting down your future plans on paper will help you to clarify and understand them. It can also help you to remember your goal even when circumstances look discouraging.

Leadership

I'd like to lead by:

"Whoever wants to become great among you must be your servant, and whoever wants to be first must be your slave—just as the Son of Man did not come to be served, but to serve."
MATTHEW 20:26–28 NIV

The qualities I look for in a leader include:

In an election, my political party of choice is:

I think the government is:

Three things I'd like to communicate to an important elected official are:

My friend says:

I'd like to lead by:

friends

Wedding Bells

What I dream my spouse might look like is:

One prayer for my future spouse is:

Five traits I'm looking for in a spouse are:

This is how I'd like to propose/be proposed to:

My vision of an ideal wedding is:

My ideal honeymoon would be in:

My friend says:

Five traits I'm looking for in a spouse are:

friends

this is who I want to be

Marriage

Wives, understand and support your husbands in ways that show your support for Christ. The husband provides leadership to his wife the way Christ does to his church, not by domineering but by cherishing.

EPHESIANS 5:22–23 THE MESSAGE

The age I think is a good age to get married is:

Three things I want to do before I get married are:

What I think about a couple living together before getting married is:

What I think being married will be like is:

My friend says:

Three things I want to do before I get married are:

What I think being married will be like is:

this is who I want to be

friends

The elements that I think are important in
marriage (besides love) are:

Three rules in my marriage about arguments will be:

The best marriage I have ever witnessed is:

As good as you feel when
you fall in love, your
feelings will come and go
with changing circum-
stances, shifting moods,
and difficult times. Trust
us. It happens.

Sometimes your feelings
will change for no appar-
ent reason. Don't be
alarmed. Keep a level
head, try to work through
the problem, and keep
the lines of communica-
tion open. Most of all,
never think about giving
up. Here's where marriage
becomes an incredibly
important factor.

The idea is this: The
sacrament of marriage
(that means the sacred
covenant) should become
so important to the two
people involved that
nothing will be able to
tear it apart. A marriage
with that kind of com-
mitment will not only
keep love together, but it
will help love grow.

FROM *SIMPLE MATTERS*
BY BRUCE AND STAN

this is who I want to be

I think the hardest thing about being
married will be:

The worst marriage I have ever witnessed is:

> I will love you like God,
> because of God, mighted
> by the power of God. I will
> stop expecting your love,
> demanding your love,
> trading for your love, gam-
> ing for your love. I will
> simply love. I am giving
> myself to you, and tomor-
> row I will do it again.
>
> FROM *BLUE LIKE JAZZ*
> BY DONALD MILLER

I (choose one) think/don't think having God in the
center of your marriage is important because:

I think couples divorce because:

I'd like to celebrate my fiftieth wedding anniversary by:

When I see old married couples together, it makes me feel:

marriage

Children

I (choose one) plan/don't plan to have children.

I want _____ kids: _____ boys and _____ girls.

Names I like include:

I'd like to decorate the nursery like:

I think the best things about having children are:

I think the keys to keep from spoiling a child are:

The things my parents did right that I will pass along to my children are:

I will discipline my child by:

I think children are the most fun at _____ years old because:

Toys my kids have to have include:

Toys my kids will never have include:

I think the most challenging things about having children are:

I (choose one) will/won't tell my children all my secrets because:

What I think of raising a child with only one parent is:

My friend says:

I think children are the most fun at _____ years old because:

friends

I think the most challenging things about having children are:

I (choose one) will/won't tell my children all my secrets because:

If my child was born with a handicap, I would feel:

If my child didn't like the things I like, I would feel:

What I will tell my children about God is:

What I will tell my children about love is:

My prayer for the child I might someday have is:

children

> The only artists for whom I would make way are—children. For me the paintings of children belong side by side with the works of the masters.
> HENRY MILLER

Travel

The journey, not the arrival, matters; the voyage, not the landing.
PAUL THEROUX

My favorite place to go so far is:

I prefer traveling by:

The place I most want to visit is:

Because:

Five places I want to travel to are:

Three people I'd like to have as traveling companions are:

My friend says:

The place I most want to visit is:

Because:

Five places I want to travel to are:

Three things to do when stuck in an airport are:

The best touristy things to do when traveling are:

Friends I've made traveling include:

The coolest conversation with a stranger on a trip occurred in:
The story is:

My favorite souvenirs to pick up when I travel are:

My favorite photo from a trip is of:

this is who I want to be

For by him were all things created, that are in heaven, and that are in earth, visible and invisible, whether they be thrones, or dominions, or principalities, or powers: all things were created by him, and for him.
COLOSSIANS 1:16 KJV

Aging

I recognize time passing because:

The difference between being older and being more mature is:

When I think about getting older, I think:

The cool thing about being older is:

The most valuable lesson I've learned from
a senior adult is:

You younger men, accept
the authority of the elders.
And all of you, serve each
other in humility, for
"God sets himself against
the proud, but he shows
favor to the humble."
So humble yourselves
under the mighty power
of God, and in his good
time he will honor you.
Give all your worries
and cares to God, for
he cares about what
happens to you.
1 PETER 5:5–7 NLT

this is who I want to be

When my parents get older, I'd like
to help them by:

How do you seize the day?
First build upon the knowledge you have that God has
worked in your life in the
past. Since God "never
changes or casts shifting
shadows" (James 1:17 NLT),
you can have confidence that
He will continue to work in
every detail of your life.
Second, have faith that God
has secured your future—
no matter what happens.
He has given you hope.

FROM *GOD IS IN THE SMALL
STUFF (AND IT ALL MATTERS)*
BY BRUCE AND STAN

Five things on my to-do list before I die are:

My friend says:

When I think about getting older, I think:

The most valuable lesson I've learned from a senior adult is:

this is who I want to be

Change the World

Live your beliefs and you can turn the world around.

HENRY DAVID THOREAU

My perfect world would look like:

If I could change five things in the world, I'd change:

I think the best way to see change happen in people is by:

The thing I have to work on in myself is this issue of belief. Gandhi believed Jesus when He said to turn the other cheek. Gandhi brought down the British Empire, deeply injured the caste system, and changed the world. Mother Teresa believed Jesus when He said everybody was priceless, even the ugly ones, the smelly ones, and Mother Teresa changed the world by showing them that a human being can be selfless. Peter finally believed the gospel after he got yelled at by Paul. Peter and Paul changed the world by starting small churches in godless towns.

FROM *BLUE LIKE JAZZ* BY DONALD MILLER

this is who I want to be

Ideas I believe can change the world are:

What I can do for the environment is:

What I can do for the poor is:

What I can do for the sick is:

What I can do for those who need great love is:

Then Jesus, looking at him, loved him, and said to him, "One thing you lack: Go your way, sell whatever you have and give to the poor, and you will have treasure in heaven; and come, take up the cross, and follow Me."

MARK 10:21 NKJV

My friend says:

My perfect world would look like:

If I could change five things in the world, I'd change:

this is who I want to be

friends

What I think it means to serve is:

Today I will make a difference and it will be:

One day I will make difference in the world and it will be:

this is who I want to be

From **I Believe:** Servanthood—Five Questions to Consider

- Would I dare to get out of my comfort zone for a couple of weeks during a mission trip. . .or for a church outreach?

- Would I dare to let God use me in a way that could change a life forever?

- Am I willing to say, "Break me, Lord. Use me in ways that stretch way beyond my imagination"?

- Do I care about those in need: the hurting, the hungry, the lonely?

- Am I willing to sacrifice my time—even my money—to impact a life for eternity?

my personal journaling

Do not let kindness
and truth leave you;
bind them around your neck,
write them on the tablet of your
heart. So you will find favor and
good repute in the sight of God
and man.

Proverbs 3:3 NASB

_____

_____

_____

_____

_____

_____

_____

_____

_____

_____

_____

_____

_____

_____

_____

_____

_____

My Personal Journaling

_____

_____

_____

_____

_____

_____

_____

_____

_____

_____

_____

_____

_____

_____

_____

_____

_____

My Personal Journaling

My Personal Journaling

My Personal Journaling

My Personal Journaling

My Personal Journaling

_____

_____

_____

_____

_____

_____

_____

_____

_____

_____

_____

_____

_____

_____

_____

_____

My Personal Journaling

My Personal Journaling

My Personal Journaling

_____

_____

_____

_____

_____

_____

_____

_____

_____

_____

_____

_____

_____

_____

_____

_____

_____

My Personal Journaling

My Personal Journaling

My Personal Journaling

_____

_____

_____

_____

_____

_____

_____

_____

_____

_____

_____

_____

_____

_____

_____

_____

_____

My Personal Journaling

my goal list

_____

_____

_____

_____

For we are His workmanship,
created in Christ Jesus for
good works, which God
prepared beforehand so that
we would walk in them.

EPHESIANS 2:10 NASB

_____

_____

_____

_____

_____

_____

_____

_____

_____

_____

_____

_____

my prayer list

I thank my God in all my
remembrance of you, always
offering prayer with joy in
my every prayer for you all.
PHILIPPIANS 1:3–4 NASB

My Prayer List

My Prayer List

My Prayer List

_____

_____

_____

_____

_____

_____

_____

_____

_____

_____

_____

_____

_____

_____

_____

_____

_____

_____

_____

_____

My Prayer List

my contacts

contacts

O love the LORD, all you His
godly ones! The LORD preserves
the faithful and fully recompenses
the proud doer. Be strong and let
your heart take courage,
all you who hope in the LORD.
PSALMS 31:23–24 NASB

Name: _____

Home phone: _____

Mobile: _____

E-mail: _____

Screen names: _____

Address: _____

Birthday: _____

Name: _____

Home phone: _____

Mobile: _____

E-mail: _____

Screen names: _____

Address: _____

Birthday: _____

My Contacts

Name: _____

Home phone: _____

Mobile: _____

E-mail: _____

Screen names: _____

Address: _____

Birthday: _____

Name: _____

Home phone: _____

Mobile: _____

E-mail: _____

Screen names: _____

Address: _____

Birthday: _____

Name: _____

Home phone: _____

Mobile: _____

E-mail: _____

Screen names: _____

Address: _____

Birthday: _____

My Contacts

Name: _____

Home phone: _____

Mobile: _____

E-mail: _____

Screen names: _____

Address: _____

Birthday: _____

Name: _____

Home phone: _____

Mobile: _____

E-mail: _____

Screen names: _____

Address: _____

Birthday: _____

Name: _____

Home phone: _____

Mobile: _____

E-mail: _____

Screen names: _____

Address: _____

Birthday: _____

My Contacts

Name: _____

Home phone: _____

Mobile: _____

E-mail: _____

Screen names: _____

Address: _____

Birthday: _____

Name: _____

Home phone: _____

Mobile: _____

E-mail: _____

Screen names: _____

Address: _____

Birthday: _____

Name: _____

Home phone: _____

Mobile: _____

E-mail: _____

Screen names: _____

Address: _____

Birthday: _____

Sources

Barbour Publishing, Inc. expresses its appreciation to all those who generously gave permission to reprint copyrighted material. Diligent effort has been made to identify, locate, contact, and secure permission to use copyrighted material. If any permissions or acknowledgments have been inadvertently omitted or if such permissions were not received by the time of publication, the publisher would sincerely appreciate receiving complete information so that correct credit can be given in future editions.

Barnhill, Carla. "I Should Have Been Dead." *Campus Life,* Jul/Aug 1998, Vol. 57, No. 1.

Bickel, Bruce and Stan Jantz. *Simple Matters.* Uhrichsville, Ohio: Promise Press, 2001.

Bickel, Bruce and Stan Jantz. *God Is in the Small Stuff (and it all matters).* Uhrichsville, Ohio: Promise Press, 2000.

Espeland, Pamela. *Life Lists for Teens.* Minneapolis, Minn.: Free Spirit, 2003.

Harris, Joshua. *Boy Meets Girl.* Sisters, Ore.: Multnomah, 2000.

Hertz, Todd. "The Frightening Truth About Scary Movies." *Campus Life,* Vol. 62, No. 4.

Lamott, Anne. *Bird by Bird.* New York: Anchor, 1994.

Manning, Brennan. *The Ragamuffin Gospel.* Sisters, Ore.: Multnomah, 1990, 2000.

Mathewes-Green, Frederica. "Drawing the Big Picture." *The Christian Reader,* Jul/Aug 2003, Vol. 41, No. 4.

Mother Teresa, *Mother Teresa: Contemplative in the Heart of the World.* Ann Arbor: Servant Publications, 1985.

Miller, Donald. *Blue Like Jazz.* Nashville, Tenn.: Thomas Nelson, 2003.

No author listed. "Playing it Safe." *Campus Life,* Nov/Dec 2000, Vol. 59, No. 4.

Ross, Michael. "Are You Gaming Wisely?" *Breakaway,* Jan 2002, Vol. 13, No. 1.

Schweer, Christie. "Never Thin Enough." *Campus Life,* Sept/Oct, Vol. 61, No. 2.

Stafford, Tim. "A Second Chance at Virginity?" *Campus Life,* Jan/Feb 2001, Vol. 59, No. 6.

Tirabassi, Becky. *Let Faith Change Your Life.* Nashville, Tenn.: Thomas Nelson, 1997.

About the Authors

Terry Brown is a nursing professional and the creator of children's and youth products including the "Communicate Christ" line and the "Today's Girls" series. She has three teenage sons and lives in east central Indiana.

Shannon Hill is a publishing industry professional, serving in publicity, marketing, editing, and product development roles. Her current title is Editor-at-Large. She is the author of several gift books and one children's novel. When not living out of a suitcase or backpack, she lives in Ohio.

If you enjoyed

This Is Who I Am,

check out

Communicate and I Believe

Communicate

Christianity is more than a lifestyle. It's a relationship with the Creator of the universe—and that's worth passing along. Especially for teens, *Communicate—Experience Him. Share Him* focuses on the two-part reality of godly living—knowing Christ in a personal, intimate way, and telling others about Him by word and deed. *Communicate* will help to equip the "new generation" to live out the Great Commission.

ISBN 1-59310-020-5
$7.97

I Believe

A unique Bible promise book designed to encourage new teenage believers and seekers.

ISBN 1-58660-842-8
$4.97

Visit www.communicatechrist.com

Available wherever Christian books are sold.